The New Age of Christ

The New Age of Christ

It is Time to Awaken

By Cheryl Yale-Bruedigam

©2017, 2020 Cheryl Yale-Bruedigam.
All Rights Reserved. 2nd Edition
ISBN 9798681397830

Cover art by Vladimir Menkov. 2010. GNU Free Documentation License. Pammakaristos Church - Main Dome of Parekklesion - Jesus Christ.

Other books by Cheryl Yale-Bruedigam:

What If We Are the Angels?
The Medieval Women's Dictionary
Choose Life, Choose Light
For Today: A Woman's Journal

Order at cherylyalebruedigam.blogspot.com

WomensLight Media, USA

This book is dedicated to Jesus Christ; the man, the embodiment of God, the bringer of love and the heart of us all.

In blessings given us through the ages
Is the Loving Light in which He came.
Do we seek that Light within our hearts?
Or do we, simply, follow a name?~ cb

Table of Contents

Introduction	11
Chapter 1 - Fresh Perspectives	19
Chapter 2 - Reconstructing Our Perceptions	30
Chapter 3 - Unlocking the Christ Within	46
Chapter 4 - Identifying with the Savior	58
Chapter 5 - Experiencing the Change	65
Chapter 6 - Turning Things Around	87
Chapter 7 - Rationing the Word	94
Chapter 8 - Our Awakening World	101
Conclusion	106

Preface

"Howbeit when he, the Spirit of truth, is come, he will guide you into all truth: for he shall not speak of himself; but whatsoever he shall hear, [that] shall he speak: and he will shew you things to come." John 16:13

This is the second edition of this book. In hindsight, it was my crossing from the New Age into Christianity. It was Jesus butting His head through the years and layers of misinterpreted and misguided teachings through which I had poured.

It has been my intent to take my time with the writing of this book to search for the truth where it may be found, both within and from the few external resources that I trust. I have written and re-written on this book multiple times for over eight years. When I first perceived the idea, I had not yet begun to cross the bridge. Then, when I began writing, I was in the middle of the crossing, which looking back, was like trying to write about a vast river, describing it's reaches all the while actually being *in* the middle of the river. Now, in this final writing, I write from where I stand, upon the sacred shore in view of the light of Christ's eternity. I write this for those who have also yet to cross but continue seeking for that one seemingly elusive truth they have yet to find. I write to assure you that it is there, but it is not necessarily as you may have perceived. It is so much more when we decide to meet Christ with an open mind; when we decide to explore His teachings with an open mind as if never read or heard. I write to assist those who linger lost, to go ahead and take that step to cross the bridge to Christ.

Obviously, I am not the first to focus either on just the teachings of Christ or the concept of Christ consciousness. *The Jefferson Bible,* or *The Life and Morals of Jesus of Nazareth,* as it is formally titled, was a book constructed by Thomas Jefferson and is certainly one example of a work with a strict and simple focus on the teachings of Jesus. I do not propose to place myself in the company of such spiritually evolved and intelligent authors, however the notion to write the book was divinely given to me and it is never really a good idea to argue with, or ignore, the desires or directives of the Holy Spirit.

Whatever you take away from *The New Age of Christ*, it is my sincerest hope that you take with you the spirit of the truth and the way to understanding, consciousness, and enlightenment through Jesus Christ.

Cheryl Yale-Bruedigam, New Mexico, August 2020

Introduction

The New Age of Christ is based on exploring the idea of uniting with Christ within and becoming Christ-like in our physical daily lives, through the actual teachings of Christ; digging to the root meanings, re-evaluating misconstrued perceptions and moving forward into the dawn of a new light in Christ, a new age of Christ. This study is not about Christianity, nor is it about *new age*, it is about Christ, the teachings of Christ and our perceptions as we awaken to Him.

The New Age of Christ is a dedicated commitment to the rebirth and awakening to His spirit in order to heal humanity, the planet and all living things through Christ as we evolve into a new enlightened era. When finally we have achieved one love, Christ will have returned. "This is my commandment, that ye love one another as I have loved you." John 15:12 (KJV)

As I said, this study is not about new age philosophy or reconstructing the teachings of Christ but rather reconstructing our *perceptions* of Christ and the teachings from which we have become so far removed. Jesus Christ yesterday, today and forever, as the saying goes. It is not Christ who has become outdated, it is our perception. We need to listen to and do what he said, but first we must allow it within and then we have to understand it. The understanding is where we need transformation.

We need a spiritual revolution but not from the pulpit, from within. Fire and brimstone is not the way to opening hearts. It has not worked thus far and it is not going to work in future generations. We need the second coming of Christ but we need the return within; within us, within our minds and hearts and spirits, and within humanity and the collective consciousness. We need to awaken to Christ within.

Our spirituality and relationship to God, to Christ, has been kept in a box. We have not been allowed to free our understanding and fully open up to Christ. Our ideas, interpretations, and perceptions about Christ have been force-fed through the mold melded by others for the sake of control rather than the sake of personal growth. If we step out and try to think otherwise, then we are being blasphemous. It is imperative for anyone wanting to follow Christ, especially if they never have, to come into His teachings with a complete open mind.

The Bible is open to interpretation. It has been interpreted over and over throughout the centuries and is all that we have to go on in understanding Christ and His teachings.

Can anyone achieve spiritual union with Christ, Yes, with the willingness one will advance because the Spirit is already with us, in us. The Spirit never leaves us; it is we who leave the Spirit by simply closing it off. We are born as children of God, but we drift away. It is our commitment to Him that revives who we truly are and once having made this commitment, the Holy Spirt returns and descends upon us just as the Bible tells us.

The yogic and Buddhist teachings of meditation enabled me to allow the opening to occur through which I was able to begin to receive the spirit of Christ. I had cycled through all of the spirit-seeking means available, philosophies, deities, but it was Jesus Christ who beckoned and showed me the way. It is the opening of the heart, and for me, the doorway in was through meditation. If you are true at heart and so desire the way, Christ will open the door.

What do you want to call it? We believe that which resonates within us. To some it is one thing, to others something else, mostly due to cultural conditioning. They say many paths lead to the source. I spent over two decades in my search after having been raised in the Methodist Church. It never seemed quite enough for me and there were many aspects of Christianity I just could not buy into because I did not have the broad spiritual foundation that I needed to understand and interpret the teachings, the symbolisms, and the mythological archetypes.

After going to college as well as continuing to study on my own, and studying many religions including Buddhism and Hindu, Native American and nature religions, plus mythology, some psychology and world literature, I had then laid the foundation I really needed to come back and pick up with my understanding of Christ and His teachings. My search went from Christianity to nature religions, mythology, to Hindu to Buddhism and back to Christ, the typical hero's journey, bringing what I learned back to my realm to apply to, and understand, my world; in this case, my spiritual world, my soul, my very being.

Though I found truths in all religions, I also found flaws, things that just didn't hold water. I took those concepts that resonated within and discarded the rest and moved on. Some things I labeled as pure bunk, others integrated within, becoming a part of my foundation; this came later though and yet still later I realized that even in all these little truths I had picked along the way, they were just a bunch of different things in my basket.

Combined they still gave me nothing concrete, nothing to catch me when I fell and later I was to fall hard. But that's another book.

In the beginning of my spiritual search I had pretty much labeled Christianity as bunk because as I said, I did not have the literate foundation to really understand so much in terms of symbolism. Now after studying and understanding many other great spiritual leaders and religions, it is like a whole new door has opened toward the understanding of Christ. This is where the appeal is, and should be, in Christ, though quite honestly, the church itself these days has little appeal to many people. They sit for an hour a week listening and singing and praying then it is back to business as usual for most. I know that churches do of course offer much more for those willing, but it is just not interesting to many, especially younger people. They see it as outdated, and this is a terrible loss and an area which we somehow need to get past so that we may begin to revive our need for God and His love in our lives.

What people need to realize is that the appeal, the mystique, lies within *them* in conjunction with Christ because that's where *He* is. Buddha showed me this and Buddha is very cool and I believe many people perceive him as so but I do not think Christ has that same perception because of how the church has handled and presented the options. We are not really shown that there is a much deeper meaning in it all.

Have you been down to the alter? Forgiven? Reborn? What happened? Did you really experience a change or just a mental relief? Were you a changed person from then on? Did you feel the inner heart open and truly receive the Holy Spirit? Or did you revert right back to your old patterns a few days or a week or a year later? If so, this is what you need to understand: there is a whole spiritual world waiting for you, already inside you, you only need to ask for the opening to Christ who is already waiting.

There are many roads to the Spirit steeped in religion, culture, nature, psychology, and mysticism worldwide. It is important to realize these universal paths and archetypes that lead to the inner Spirit, to the union with God and all that is, and their relation to each other because ultimately when one is truly seeking the truth, the truth will be given by God. The more we know and understand and share, the stronger, more compassionate and more enlightened we become for humanity and this is a foundational teaching of Christ. It is time to look inward to move forward outwardly. Union with Christ, and with each other, is needed to bring us as individuals and as a collective, to a peaceful and harmonious place in existence and beyond.

Many seek enlightenment in various ways; Buddhism, Christianity, Islam, Judaism, Hinduism, nature and tribal religions all share pathways to the inner Spirit if one is willing to allow the opening to appear and it is this opening that will lead us to the ultimate truth in Christ. That is what happened for me. A true seeker leaves no rock unturned, possesses an open mind and is able to process and sift through the mounds of information for the grains of truth that lie beneath, but once the opening has been made, discernment is then given as a gift of the Holy Spirit and we are able to move into the inner circle per say.

Eighty-six percent of the world's population considers themselves to be spiritual. If this eighty-six percent's beliefs were working there should be very few problems in the world. In many cases though, these beliefs are not working; perhaps due to a lack of effort, faith, guidance or true desire. Many people have turned away from organized religion due to fanaticism, church control, and outdated dogma. Extremity in any direction is not positive for it closes the mind and allows no room for growth or truth. What we need is the way to the Spirit in the heart. The teachings and compassion of Christ offer the way.

In past teachings we are told what He said; what we are not told is how to get there; how to find the opening, allow the opening where the compassion of Christ may enter wherein we may achieve union with Christ and where we too may live in the kingdom of heaven within. I do not think we are fully told the amount of real spiritual effort that will be required of us. The teachings of Christ have sometimes been compromised and condensed into a social format of ease which is sadly not always lasting and many turn away. It is not until we unravel the depths of truth to see and understand what was truly given in detail (Christ living within us, receipt of the fruits of the Holy Spirit), that we can achieve that which is set before us. It takes work, commitment and most of all, the desire to be with God.

If you are unsure, or have yet to achieve a union with Christ, I invite you to explore the teachings of Christ with me in a new and fresh look at what Christ truly offers, not through the interpretation of bureaucratic dogma but from the soul-level. There is much to learn and interpret with a fresh viewpoint.

If you have not yet found your path to the Christ, isn't it about time you did? As He says, "For what profit is it to a man if he gains the whole world, and loses his own soul?" Matthew 16:26 (KJV)

Chapter 1 - Fresh Perspectives

The teachings and understanding of Christ with the goal of achieving union with Him as the way to the spiritual Father have been so misconstrued and misunderstood that any resemblance of the original message has been completely lost to the world today buried beneath piles of history and complicated ritual and dogma. It is therefore critical that the teachings of Christ be revisited with an open mind and heart that those who choose to follow will gain the truth of understanding as they move forward into the light and achieve attainment of this spiritual union with Christ.

Are we talking about Christ as the literal son of God or as consciousness? They are singular in meaning for we are all the children of God. Regardless of whether you believe that Christ is the Son of God or a prophet, whatever the truth, we will never know as far as scientific proof and data; and even if He did return in the flesh and appeared on Oprah, he would be lumped in as another alternative or new-age flake. It is not important as to the historical facts for they are varied, arguable, unproven and many, but rather what is important are two things: the spiritual teachings themselves and achieving union with Christ through these teachings.

We are sent here in the physical to experience the magic of life in the physical. We have the choice to say yes to this, to open our inner eye to this, or to ignore it and refuse the growth, the lessons, and the evolution of Spirit. And in doing so, we are not just denying our self; we are denying the Spirit, the Creator, who gave us this opportunity for Him to experience life in the physical. This is the sin against Spirit and against the magic of life itself. If Christ were the son of God, then this is what was happening, and if he was simply an enlightened son of man, this is still what was happening. Either way, the Spirit lived in the flesh through Him. We are all given this choice.

The argument of whether Christ was a son of man or the son of God is not what is important; what matters are the teachings and the achievement. What matters is what you are able to take away from it and what you are able to become. All the arguments of doctrine are simply surface and superficial, egoic and transmuted. The point is two-fold; does it bring you to being a good person, have you achieved the Divine? That is all that matters. The arguments are a distraction from finding and experiencing the truth. We can argue from here to eternity and nothing will be solved. The only solution is to put away the argument and go within while at the same time experiencing external life to the fullest. And it does not matter which side of the fence you are on, whether you go to church on Sunday or whether you live an alternative life and are working to free Tibet, if you are not living Christ-like, you are not getting it. You must be awakened to Christ within.

We must allow ourselves the extension of true and deep understanding and the right to choose. We exert to get to the truth but many barriers stand in the way: time, culture and language to name a few. But it is our inherit right as children of light, to believe and to follow these great teachings that have been so diminished and misconstrued. All are welcome and all are of the light. We are here to achieve enlightenment, union with Christ. There are some who can attain this on their own but for most the ways and the teachings were brought forth to follow and enact and these teachings are in the Gospels of Jesus Christ.

"Jesus saith unto him, I am the way, the truth, and the life: no man cometh unto the Father, but by me," John 14.6 (KJV), with "Father" being the source of All that Is. It is our claim to understanding that negates this with reprehension to all who seek the Spirit for it is just and good to all that believe rather than just to those whose own interpretations have misconstrued the teachings.

We need to learn to see Christ from within, from the inner Spirit, not from the external perceptions put upon us. Working with the teachings of Christ and moving toward union with Christ helps those who have been unable to "connect" or who have drifted away from traditional belief systems. Getting back to the root of the Spirit, as Christ lived, as Christ was, as Christ taught, is the true purpose.

When Jesus spoke again to the people, he said, "I am the light of the world. Whoever follows me will never walk in darkness, but will have the light of life." John 8.12 (KJV)

Decline in Religion or Spirituality?

Church-going is on the decline in America and it serves to take a brief look at why this has happened. Let us explore the origin of *church*.

Middle English *chirche*, from Old English *cirice*, ultimately from Late Greek *kyriakon*, from Greek, neuter of *kyriakos* of the lord, from *kyrios* lord, master; akin to Sanskrit *śūra* hero, warrior
First Known Use: before 12th century. (Websters)
One important thing to look at here is that the word "church" did not even exist in Biblical times

nor did churches. The original word from which it does derive is *kyriakos*, "of the lord" and the word chosen for translation was *ecclesia* which translates from the Greek "called" and "out" meaning those *called out*.

Quoting from the Oxford Universal English Dictionary on the word *ecclesia*, ": Ecclesia [mediaeval Latin, and Greek - from: SUMMONED] -A regularly convoked assembly, especially the general assembly of Athenians. Later, the regular word for church."

The point being that church did not exist. Church as it is known today has become a turn-off for many people. What was meant was addressing those who had been called out by the Holy Spirit and the teachings of Jesus Christ who then formed themselves into followers in one civil body, renouncing Caesar as king, following Christ instead, giving up their possessions and living together as one under the teachings of Christ.

Translations

According to Brian Knowles of godward.org, some scholars still believe that the daily language of Christ was Galilean Aramaic brought back by the Jews from Babylon. Others now believe in light of new research that he spoke and taught in Hebrew.

Others still say he spoke and taught in Greek. Regardless, translations pose one of our biggest obstacles in seeking the truth therefore for further translations, we must use the heart and that which resonates within. With that in mind, using a King James Bible or the Catholic Douay version or the best place to start because they are about as old and as far back as we can begin. Modern translations can then be made useful for interpretations.

Cool vs. Un-cool Perceptions

Today we are living in a high-tech/low-spirit world. The generations coming up are suffering severely from a lack of spiritual contact with God, spiritual guidance and with nature. I have witnessed this in my own children, try as we did to give them a spiritual understanding and closeness to the natural world, I fear that technology won out. The younger generations really need something to grab onto. As it is, they are seeking what little spiritual connection they may through the media. Their perception of religion and church is bad, and understandably so, it was the same for many of us in my generation in the sixties and seventies. It is un-cool to them in a world where "cool" has become everything. You are cool if you have the latest this or that high-tech toy. You are cool if you are texting on your cell phone. What I am saying to these younger people is the soul is cool, and hey, guess what, so is Christ. It is the presentation, the perception that is not cool. It is our own lack of understanding that is not cool. We can change that.

In watching a documentary on the life of Christ, I saw his life as the hero's journey as laid out by Joseph Campbell. The life of Christ reads like any popular epic. In our lifetimes, we have come to relate Jesus Christ to overly strict church regimes and this relation has laid the very foundation for how many perceive Christ, incorrectly. Just imagine Christ with the same presentation and representation that an epic such as *Lord of the Rings* had. While watching the documentary (this is how my mind perceived it), I saw the story so clearly in this Hollywood epic style. Not to cheapen but to enlighten, especially the youth, that Christ *was* cool (and still is) and he did indeed live and travel the hero's journey and that His teachings are valuable and enlightening when perceived in the right understanding.

Most people do not venture out of their hobbit hole onto the hero's journey of spiritual growth. Many do not even seek any spiritual growth, while others are content with merely the attendance of a weekly service, thinking this is all that is necessary to achieve union with Christ. I began my own journey in weekly service but left the pews and alter behind to search the world and its cultures for the truth wherever it could be found through masters of all ancient religions and study, and most of all within myself. In coming full circle and returning to to Christ, I was able to bring back what I learned and apply the knowledge and understanding to the teachings of Christ. I am not saying that you need to go out and experience all the obvious mistakes I made in pursuit of the Spirit, no indeed, but it is a blessing that I can relate these experiences and share them in hopes of getting you closer to where you need to be, without all the confusion and misunderstanding. Grabbing at truths here and there served no overall purpose yet it did provide a depth that I otherwise did not have when I began which served to further increase my desire for unity and for understanding.

All of the visual imagery that we have in our heads about Christ came from the artists of the Medieval and Renaissance periods. We have allowed these depictions to largely shape our views and perceptions. It is not to say that these are not beautiful depictions, and that some may have been spiritually intuited, but we must also be willing to leave an open space in the mind in order to seek and find the truth.

According to Joseph Campbell, "There is a Hindu tantric saying, nādevo devam arcayet, 'by none but a god shall a god be worshipped.' The deity of one's worship is a function of one's own state of mind. But it is also a product of one's culture. Catholic nuns do not have visions of the Buddha, nor do Buddhist nuns have visions of Christ. Ineluctably, the image of any god beheld—whether interpreted as beheld in heaven or as beheld at çakra 6–will be of a local ethnic idea historically conditioned, a metaphor, therefore, and thus to be recognized as transparent to transcendence. Remaining fixed to its form, whether with simple faith or in saintly vision, is therefore to remain in mind historically bound and attached to an appearance." (Joseph Campbell, The Inner Reaches of Outer Space: Metaphor as Myth and as Religion, p.39)

Based on this thinking, the images with which we are enculturated are likely to stay with us but we need to at least allow for a fresh and personal perspective. We must continue to grow in our understanding of Christ. We must remain openminded so that He will be able to reveal His truth within us.

Have we not evolved in our thinking and understanding of Christ, of God, of spiritual elements? Growth is natural, evolution is natural, and it is desirable that we strive to move forward in our understanding and in our ability to achieve spiritual union with Christ, for without it, we are sure to stagnate in both our thinking and in our spiritual growth. If one digs deep enough, one will find mysticism within Catholicism, but Protestantism does not seem to have an understanding that something deeper may, and indeed does, exist. As the Bible says, the true mystery is that Christ lives within us. How deeply are we willing to allow and explore and live this truth?

All that we have discovered through the ages and have passed down, preserved in writing, oral tradition and whichever means that we may, has been given to us through our understanding and communion with the Spirit. It did not give us all it had, then just stopped and said, *well there you go, that's it in a nutshell.* No, there is always more to learn, more to understand, more to seek. Achieving our union with Christ is just the beginning of our understanding. It is the tapping of the vein. Once done, then we are able to grow and learn and move through Spirit as it becomes us, as we become it and we open more and more to this new state of being. Christ's teachings were the way to achieve this so that we could then begin our journey of spiritual growth and understanding. We have not learned all there is to know. He came, He showed us how to achieve the path to "heaven" but it is up to us to move ourselves forward in learning, both as individuals, and as a collective human race and soul.

Treating the teachings as though they are all there are and not striving to move deeper into them is an insult to the teachings themselves for they were gifted to us with exactly that in mind. The teachings were given us so that we would follow *the way*, so that we would *have* a way, to learn, to understand and to further execute all that waits in Spirit. Each of us sees in various degrees from the perspective of ego, depending upon the baggage and experience we carry. To see clearly, one must look from the soul. Christ gave us the teachings to be able to do this, to see from the soul. It is up to us now to look further with a fresh new perspective toward learning, evolving and understanding as much as we may about our union with Christ and the Holy Spirit.

Chapter 2 - Reconstructing Our Perceptions

It is likely that every belief and philosophy began as a single truth given by the God to the person who realized it (wise men and teachers such as Buddha, Christ, Krishna, and so on), but each of these truths of wisdom and teachings were then built upon, argued, manipulated (some omitted, others rearranged, all to suit the ego and control of those in power) and turned into man-made doctrine.

It is up to us individually to seek out the one seed of truth, find the innate wisdom, feel the peace that resonates within us, and come to the light of understanding using these original teachings coupled with our own heartfelt intuition. This is what the teachings are for: to propel our own growth and understanding rather than to mindlessly repeat passages while remaining closed up inside a spiritual box. This was not the intention of our great spiritual teachers. They would encourage exploration, debate and truth-seeking as these were what brought them to their own understanding from wherein they derived their teachings. You can bet that what has happened to the teachings of Jesus Christ was not His intent, nor did He intend to be worshipped. He came to share the teachings wherein we might reach "the Father," within us and that we might worship the Father *through* Him.

Let us consider that all of the world's major religions originated in some part of the East whether near, middle or far. Judaism, Islam, Christianity, Buddhism and Hinduism all originated in the Eastern world. All of these religions share some common beliefs and universal teachings yet the further west these religions have traveled, the more distorted and possibly misunderstood they have become as in the case of Protestant Christianity. It broke apart, filtering and changing until it no longer resembles anything of original Christianity. We interpret and perceive these teachings today based on a contemporary Western mindset. Christ was of an Eastern mindset; He and the teachers and prophets of the other major religions were all of an Eastern mindset and influenced by commonalities of the region. It is up to us to find our way back to these early and original teachings and understandings and apply them to the search within the inner self toward unity with Christ. Yet we cannot do this until we return to the root of His teachings, to the original meanings, and the current climate makes this difficult because of the distortion that has evolved within Christianity. The best way to remedy this, is to read the Gospels for our self, with an open mind, without past associations of various dominations.

It is time to take back the teachings of Christ so that true Christians may once again be proud to claim their rightful representation and walk together in love. There are true Christians who are ashamed to admit they are Christians because of what has been done in Christ's name. It is time to walk in love for humanity, as Christ taught. We are all children of God. It is time to restore the image of Christ to its true nature of our own human consciousness through the consciousness of Christ and His love.

What we are taught to do to find union with Christ verses what we need to be doing are completely different things: Just say *saved*. We are told to say our prayers, read the Bible, go to church, tithe; we are not taught on the surface in everyday life how to go within and reach union with Christ so these things do not last nor contribute to our evolution. We relate church to door-to-door salesmen and that is not what it is at all. It is not a structure, it is not a day of the week, it is the whole body of Christ. It takes really digging into the teachings, praying for understanding and spending time in contemplation for Christ to reveal His will for us. Paul spoke of immature Christians being nursed on mother's milk, and this is true. It is a process of growth and with much time and effort are we then ready for solid food wherein we experience the truth of God for ourselves.

It used to be in protestant America (with protestant's root word being *protest*) that if someone did not agree with what a preacher said, they would simply go down the road, get a building and open another church and this is one reason our views have become so far apart and so spread out from the original teachings as well as the loss of retaining any true spiritual seeking, especially if compared to the Eastern Orthodox Church or the Roman Catholic Church. Let us take a brief look at the evolution of Christianity from the original church, particularly toward western society in Protestant America:

God
Son of God
Christianity
Roman Catholics
The Church of England
Protestant Immigration to America
Breakdown and separation of denominations
Denominations with political agendas
Strife, hate, anger, discrimination
The division of Christ's teachings
Full Division
Loss of God

All of the literature available to us was written by people from their interpretations, and in later materials, their denominations. What we need to seek is Christ, not the dogma. This is what Christ was saying, the kingdom of heaven lies within. "Neither shall they say, Lo here! or, lo there! for, behold, the kingdom of God is within you." Luke 17:21 (KJV). It *is* that simple. There is wisdom in many teachings that provide underlying advancement for us but ultimately the truth lies within us in Christ. It does not matter which bridge you cross as long as you get to the other side. This book is my crossing of that bridge. It was the beginning of Christ's calling to me from within.

In researching recently, I came across the idea of the Gnostic Christ. So I decided to research Gnosticism. Though I do agree with many points, it became extremely complicated very quickly. Basically it follows the concept that union with the soul is individually received through Divine knowledge and Christ was sent here with the teachings. This is very much how I believe but then it gets into all these demi-gods and deities and a dualistic supreme being and on and on; becoming very complicated. There are writings that were found in 1945 in Egypt dating to from the first to the third century, the Nag Hammana Library.

Many whom I have studied and admire were heavily influenced by the Gnostics, like Carl Jung and William Blake. It all got me to thinking that though there may be some truths in it, anything that is over-complicated is probably not completely right spiritually speaking, rather a spiritual Aukman's Razor if you will. In my own studies I did not delve too deeply with Buddhisim or Hinduism, they became very complicated very quickly; so many deities, so much to comprehend without having been raised within those belief systems. The same holds true for all major religions, not the teachings of those they are based upon but of the complicated intricacies woven by man in the quest for spiritual understanding and even for political control. It is not to say the teachings do not work in some respects, because they obviously do in many cases. It is just to wonder why all of it needs to be so complicated.

Spirituality is just not that complicated, the teachings of Christ were not complicated. One should at least be able to sum up the main concept, the bottom line in a sentence or two with any belief system. The problem is that in humanity's struggle to understand and to get to the truth, we have so over-complicated it all to the point that it is not understandable and most people would shy away from anything so complicated, whereas it is really not complicated at all.

There is Spirit/God and our goal is to become one with that. We come to life as humans and it is our challenge to re-discover our core, our essence. We spend a lifetime doing it and then we return to that which we were. We were given the teachings through Christ to find our way home.

Sure, there is more to it than all that; what happens afterward, etc., all the usual questions: is there a divine plan, is there a judgment day, is there a heaven and a hell? Does destiny or fate exist, do we have free will? These are philosophical questions but the union with Christ itself is an action that is available to us all no matter the religion, creed or belief system, or the lack of one. In the end, regardless of the former belief system, it comes down to the individual and their own union with Christ, which is pretty simple and straightforward if one allows it.

Perhaps we over-complicate things; perhaps all we really need to do is love and when we love, we find all else that we need but getting past those love blocks is the difficult and confusing part. Life is a journey of love and God holds the key. When we can open up and let the love of Christ flow through us then everything we need emotionally and spiritually is there within us. It always was but when we become open to receiving and all the blocks begin to fall away like yesterday's tired and worn façade, we open to the flow. A lightness permeates the body and mind as the feeling of freedom and joy flow for perhaps the first time ever. Had I simply opened myself up to Christ long ago, I would have received so much more love and healing but I needed to learn the lessons I learned and it has all been in God's divine-time.

We just over-complicate so much, not only the search for love and healing but for God and religion, which when you think about it, the simple truth is that they are the same. Love/God; pretty simple.

There are those of us who also receive teachings, as did those who came before us, and the teachings we receive help ourselves and others to continue to grow and evolve spiritually. We are helpers, helping to muddle our way through what has become an extremely over-complicated and overgrown path to spiritual union.

We all have differences but we all share the same spirit, that is the spirit of God and this is what Christ came to teach. Much is not known about His life but from the teachings that remain, we can move forward into the understanding that He truly tried to put forth: to love one another, to become good hearts and souls who through doing so would enter the kingdom of heaven. This heaven is also in our hearts and minds and souls, as well as eternal life.

When someone I loved died, who had gone through the motions of Christianity, i.e., went to church on Sundays later in life, been baptized, read the Bible and thumped it all the way but did not truly live a giving, loving life, sincere in the practicing the teachings of Christ, I had a vision. After his passing he stood high upon a bridge, his papers to cross the bridge in his hand. As he held them up in what he thought was the inspection to pass, they were whipped away into the wind.

Is it my place to judge this person's life and behavior based on a vision? No, it is based on my life experience with him. He proclaimed one thing but lived another. That of course is between him and God but it showed me without a shadow of a doubt in my mind that if we do not sincerely live the teachings of Christ, we will not be allowed to cross the bridge. That much I was shown. This helped me to refresh my perspective. It is simple really: walk your talk. It is the misunderstanding and complicated dogma that sometimes make things more difficult but when understanding is brought back down to a root focus, we can then see clearly.

There are a few strongly perceived ideas from Christianity associated with Christ that are worth reviewing with a fresh perspective because sometimes they are so overly complicated that we cannot see clearly or understand the root meanings.

For instance, tithing was a Mosiac law in Biblical times, that required the Israelites to give one tenth of their produce to support the Levitical priesthood. (Leviticus 27:30-33) It is not associated with the teachings of Christ, as a matter of fact, Christ encouraged his followers to give away their belongings and it is widely known that this was in favor of a communal lifestyle. This is not to say one should not tithe or give to the church or to those in need; absolutely, but we need to know the reasoning behind it, the root behind it and understand that this is not related to an inner relationship or to living in Christ. It is more that as we progress in Christ, we will begin to naturally want to give back.

The Resurrection

One of the fundamental beliefs of Christianity is the resurrection. The resurrection is within each of us and it is up to us to receive and to allow Christ to live again within us.

From *Strong's Exhaustive Concordance*, "Resurrection is from the Greek word *Anastasis* or raised to life again, resurrection. From *anistemi*; a standing up again, i.e. (literally) a resurrection from death (individual, genitive case or by implication, (its author)), or (figuratively) a (moral) recovery (of spiritual truth) -- raised to life again, resurrection, rise from the dead, that should rise, rising again."

Whether or not the physical body of Christ actually rose, through this idea we are given the teaching to seek and allow a rebirth of Christ within our own self. "I am the resurrection, and the life: he that believeth in me, though he were dead, yet shall he live: 26 And whosoever liveth and believeth in me shall never die. Believest thou this?" John 11:25-26 (KJV).

Christ wants us to celebrate His life and teachings as this is where the true entrance to Christ lies.

Apocolypse

"But of that day and that hour knoweth no man, no, not the angels which are in heaven, neither the Son, but the Father." Mark 13:32 (KJV)

This is stated thus because our union with Christ is different for each person but as more and more individuals achieve this awakening, the collective consciousness of the human race will begin to rise.

"Armageddon" is mentioned only once in the Bible and "the battle of Armageddon" is not mentioned at all.

The one passage which does mention "Armageddon" (or more correctly, *Har-magedon*) occurs in the book of Revelation: "And the sixth angel poured out his bowl on the great river, the Euphrates; and its water was dried up, that the way might be prepared for the kings of the east. And I saw coming out of the mouth of the dragon and out of the mouth of the beast and out of the mouth of the false prophet, three unclean spirits like frogs; for they were spirits of demons, performing signs, which go out to the kings of the whole world, to gather them together for war on the great day of God, the Almighty. (Behold, I am coming like a thief. Blessed is the one who stays awake and keeps his garments, lest he walk about naked and men see his shame.) And they gathered them together to the place which in Hebrew is called Har-magedon." Revelations 16:12-16 (KJV)

Apocalypse - apokalypsis, from *apokalyptein* to uncover, from apo- + kalyptein to cover. (Webster's)

: An apocalypse (Ancient Greek: ἀποκάλυψις *apocálypsis,* from ἀπό and καλύπτω meaning 'uncovering'), translated literally from Greek, is a disclosure of knowledge, i.e., a lifting of the veil or revelation. (Wiki Apocalypse). It is not a negative term though our connotations are entirely negative, especially when viewed by those outside the spiritual realm and instead through the media, books and movies. It is a positive term, it is our awakening.

Rapture

The Full Definition of rapture:
1: an expression or manifestation of ecstasy or passion
2a : a state or experience of being carried away by overwhelming emotion

b : a mystical experience in which the spirit is exalted to a knowledge of divine things

3 often capitalized : the final assumption of Christians into heaven during the end-time according to Christian theology. (Webster's)

The term rapture is not even in the Bible and it too is a word scary to those outside the realm of spiritual living yet it should not be, it is a positive word. This is one of those areas where in reading the teachings, we must use what is imprinted upon our heart by the Holy Spirit in processing and understanding Christ's teaching.

Salvation

In looking at the second definition of salvation from Webster's, taking it out of the Christian context, it is, *2: liberation from ignorance or illusion*, and this is more applicable in the context of attaining spiritual consciousness. God's will is for our salvation. The original meaning of "will" is from the Latin for wish, or desire. God's will is for our eternal salvation therefore that can translate that the eternal will is salvation, the eternal desire is liberation from ignorance or illusion. This is what God offers us as we accept Christ and are set free of the bondage of the earthly realm and attain a

Christlike mind. We are then freed for eternity, achieving eternal salvation through Christ.

The Devil

The problem with the concept of the "devil" is that then the believer perceives the threat as external rather than also as the internal threat that it is. Therefore, rather than battle the ego, the believer is duped into thinking they are free of any self-responsibility as it is all perceived as external. Whether we want to call it the devil, the ego, the shadow-self, or even a collective force that affects us all, we must defeat our own darkness within in order to reach unity with Christ as it is this darkness that keeps the pathway to unity closed. Christ provides the measures for battle within His teachings. Paul advises us to put on the full armor of God. The helmet of salvation which protects our thoughts and mind, the breastplate of righteousness which protects our heart, the shield of faith that we may resist all dark attempts upon us, the sword of the word of God which gives us the positive words we need to overcome anything, the belt of truth in knowing that we are right in Christ's guidance and the shoes of the Gospel of peace which keep us calm and peaceful in the midst of the darkest times that we may carry that peace with us and leave it wherever we go.

The above just a few terms that need to be taken back to the root for a clearer understanding and a fresh perspective particularly in how they relate to Christ (or not) and to coming to Christ in our lives. We cannot do so with so many negative perceptions and connotations on these everyday words that are a part of the teachings.

Chapter 3 – Accepting Christ

Jesus Christ already resides within each of us. All we have to do is accept Him into our hearts to allow the opening, the way, to clear.

Turning inward is the way to a deeper understanding and connection with Christ. It is a path of seeking, it is a journey. It is the journey already prepared for us if we choose to receive it.

Is being spiritual is a simple matter? Simple yes; easy no. I read somewhere that we do not have to work at being spiritual because we already are. This is true in a way but it is also deceptive because of the psychological aspects we must break through, the cultural conditioning we must break through and the day-to-day battle we must fight against any type of negativity. Becoming and remaining spiritual does take work and effort. Just believing we are spiritual does not necessarily make it so. We are spiritual yes, but living spiritually is another matter entirely and this is where and why we need the teachings Christ provided so that we live spiritually rather than just saying we *are* spiritual and leaving it at that.

To begin, one must consciously choose to open up and to pursue a union with Christ and maintain this through daily practice because the ego, the wall, the mental chatter, all try their best to override our union with Him. It is what Christ meant when he said to take up the cross. Matthew 16:24 (KJV), "Then said Jesus unto his disciples, If any man will come after me, let him deny himself, and take up his cross, and follow me." Taking up the cross requires a lot of spiritual work and readiness, sacrifice, death of the ego and the self and preparedness to go the length, to walk your talk.

According to Got Questions Ministries, "Because the Romans forced convicted criminals to carry their own crosses to the place of crucifixion, bearing a cross meant carrying their own execution device while facing ridicule along the way to death. Therefore, 'Take up your cross and follow Me' means being willing to die in order to follow Jesus. This is called 'dying to self.' It's a call to absolute surrender. After each time Jesus commanded cross bearing, He said, 'For whoever wants to save his life will lose it, but whoever loses his life for me will save it. What good is it for a man to gain the whole world, and yet lose or forfeit his very self?' Luke 9:24-25. Although the call is tough, the reward is matchless."

The important thing here though is to understand that the cross is a metaphorical gate ton allow you to access to true spirituality and to Christ.

In terms of uniting with Christ, this is the letting the old self, the ego, die to experience rebirth within which again, takes work, readiness and effort. It is the willingness to die for Christ, meaning to let the old self die to live in unity with Christ.

To do this we must deny our selfish desires and put the will of God first. As put by David Pratt of The Gospel Way, ". . . so many people are not truly Jesus' disciples (whether or not they may claim to be His disciples): because they are not willing to make this total sacrifice [taking up the cross]."

The idea of the cross itself, though respected by many, has also become degraded in some religious circles. The cross is a sacred symbol and should not be taken or treated lightly. The wearing or display of the cross should be for those who have truly denied their self and follow in the path of Christ. It is yet one more aspect of Christianity that has been completely twisted around and abused to the point that its true meaning is near lost and unrecognizable. But one must awaken to the higher understanding to truly see this. Many of us spend our lives thinking we are living a spiritual life; I know I certainly have. It is not until we understand the true meaning of Christ's statement to take up the cross and follow Him, that we really begin to live in the consciousness of Christ and once we do this, once we act in faith and completely turn our life over to God, then we are able to come to the place of living spiritually. However we see the Spirit, through whatever cultural or mythological eyes we perceive it, it still boils down to these teachings and the living of them are the simple earnest truths. They have been taught and shared by many teachers. Some people are spiritual enough to find these teachings within their own self by developing a Christ consciousness, a Buddha consciousness, without the need of external teachers, but those are rare. Most of us need the guidance and translation of a spiritual teacher and an example to follow. Christ is this example and in taking up the cross, we are stepping out to live that example.

If Christ came to you today and told you that if you wanted to be a true Christian, that you must give up everything you have materially so that you might follow and do the work of God, would you? Are you prepared to do this? Are you willing to give up your lifestyle, your house, your cars, your credit cards and vacations and shopping sprees and all?

He has already requested this and many other things that are not being followed. It is not to say that it is His will for you to lose everything or give up everything but the question is are you *willing? The Lord is my shepherd, I shall not want.* This is what Christ tried to teach us.

He said in Luke 17:21 (KJV), 21 "Neither shall they say, Lo here! or, lo there! for, behold, the kingdom of God is within you." Pretty simply put. It means what it says and we need look no further than within. It is from the grace of God that we are given this gift. Each of us is capable of reaching the kingdom within if only we can free our hearts and minds to accept His offer.

When we allow Christ in, we achieve eternal life because we have consciously merged with the Him, with God the Spirit. Opening your heart to love is one of the first steps in moving toward this. How do we do this? How do we open the heart?

Allowing love into our lives allows us to fully experience the human existence. Most of us love our families, our spouse, our children, some friends, our pets. Some do not even have this much love. This is not the same as fully allowing love to come into our life to extend this love to all; everyone, every thing. Opening the heart is not as easy as it sounds. We have baggage; guilt, regret, fear, hurt and pain, anger, resentment, and many other dark spirits dwelling within our hearts that have taken over, taken up the space, built up walls and blocked out many forms of love. It is the extended love that we receive from God that allows us to open our hearts to share and connect with others, with all living things including our planet and the natural world upon it. This extended love also includes the love of life itself, what we do to fill our days and the feeling and love with which we do it. It includes feeling love in every moment through the higher source and staying in direct consciousness with the source, through Christ.

We block off so many feelings, so much of the human experience, and we do this for many reasons with the fear of being hurt or rejected leading the list. Another reason is to block off the pain we have felt from being hurt in the past. We harden our hearts, we close off, we turn away. Sometimes we are afraid to extend love to anything that is different or unfamiliar out of a similar fear, fear of getting hurt by the unknown and this can range from a person we have just met on our street to nations of people from whom we are different.

One way to begin to heal this block is to awaken to the connectedness of all living beings, understanding that we are all one, we are all the same. The only differences that exist are cultural, religious, and governmental across a few lines that have been drawn in order to more clearly understand the geography of our planet, but within these borders, we are still all one and the same.

If you are sincere in your spiritual search, ask to be guided to the opening of your heart so that you might receive the love of Christ that can extend to all beings. Some of the best methods to use are prayer and prayer-centered meditation

Additionally, as you sit with God, you will begin to feel the opening of the heart and the wonderful world of joy that may be received. It is said that prayer is when we talk to God, meditation is when we listen. Quiet down, go within, listen and begin to experience your connection to Christ. It is the path to God waiting right there within. All you have to do is seek and listen.

Ask in prayer for the love of Christ to fill you up with joy and then wait and watch for the magic to happen. Sincerity in prayer will get you everywhere. All the angels need is your request and they will happily begin to escort you consciously along on your journey. They have been with you all along but it is up to you to take the step, to open the door where Christ is knocking. Revelations 3:20 says, "Behold, I stand at the door, and knock: if any man hear my voice, and open the door, I will come in to him, and will sup with him, and he with me."

If you will begin to practice these t methods, prayer and prayer-centered meditation you will have made a big leap in opening the heart to connect with the love of Christ that will fill you with love for all things. Opening your heart is the first big step. Release all negativity within and there will not only be room for love but there will be infinite love. There will be awakening. Turn the negativity over to Him and be freed to awaken.

Awakening comes in many ways. There are those who experience some kind of tragedy and experience an awakening; there are those who are seeking to awaken and stumble across it in a more organic way, there are those who in the end experience a brief but magnificent awakening, there are those few who were seemingly born awake, and sadly there are those who never awaken at all.

A friend battling cancer wrote a piece recently about living each day as if it were the last. It got me to thinking, reminded me of the poem in the movie *Calendar Girls* about the older women being like flowers that bloom at the last minute; that some people spend their whole lives in darkness, only to have an explosion of light at the very end, though in some cases it is too late.

To awaken is the reason that we are here; to learn to love and appreciate life and all living things within it as well as to return to God through Christ within. We each have our own lessons to learn but we should seek to awaken so that we do not waste a single minute of our precious lives. How many of us just trudge through our days, year after year, unaware of all the love, joy and beauty that surround us? Or to the fact that there are so many doing without who need help and comfort? When we awaken, we allow Christ to live and work through us, to walk in each of us. This is how He is able to return, and when we all come Him, He will have returned.

Whether or not there are any religious beliefs involved, the point is to get there, to awaken. Why wait until it has to be forced upon you or risk it being too late or never happening at all? It is up to each of us to open our eyes and to see with our hearts; fully, and gratefully.

The kingdom of heaven lies within us. It seems a universal teaching, and if it lies within us, then we are indeed spiritual beings who can, and should, strive toward Christ-like behavior and when we begin to do this, He will be there. Once we transcend our own blocks of negativity, we can cross over and we become one with Christ.

Accepting Christ is not just about worship or just attending church, or even just believing; it is about experiencing Christ within, about being, becoming Him in likeness. Christ offers us to experience God through Him. It is about opening our consciousness to allow the Spirit in so that we in turn become Christ-like in all our ways, thoughts, actions, perceptions and behaviors. This is the incarnation of Christ; this is God become man through Christ and each man/woman in turn becoming the incarnation of Christ and of God in human form.

The moment you perceive the light, everything shifts. Accepting Christ is an attainment for living and for the understanding necessary to evolve in higher Spirit and truth. We must release all shadows and allow the darkness to turn to wisdom. Waking up is to come alive with love. The way to the Father (God) is through Christ. This may be interpreted from, "Jesus saith unto him, I am the way, the truth, and the life: no man cometh unto the Father, but by me." John 14:6 (KJV)

It is heaven that we seek. Heaven is within us, heaven is here, heaven is everywhere. If we seek to be in heaven on the other side then we must first find heaven here. Do you think that if you do not find it here, that you will find it there? Whether you look at it in simple spiritual terms or Christianity or how, it is the same universal truth. In simple spiritual terms, we must find it within, and it is such that we will take with us. If you look at it in Christian terms, in order to get to heaven, you must become a good person here, become Christ-like, and then you will be taken into heaven. Becoming Christ-like here is the same thing as finding heaven here within you because once you become Christ-like, you are in heaven on earth and you are in heaven already. It is all one and the same. Finding heaven within is salvation.

Christ walks among us in every heart that beats. It is not whether *they* behave like Christ; it is whether *we* do when we meet them.

Sometimes we try too hard to understand and process too much. Just stop trying, just be. It is OK to not know. It is OK to just be. Too much searching for understanding is draining and confusing. When you feel confusion or uncertainty, worry or fear, guilt or doubt, pull yourself back to the present moment. There is always peace within. Our fundamental servitude is to the light within. That light is lit by Christ.

Whatever your beliefs or cultural terms and definitions, if you go far enough into your spiritual practice, you too will find that Christ within is truly universal and that all of this worldly quibbling over what is right, what is wrong, is simply all wrong. Christ is universal and lives within every single one of us. It is the God-spark energy source within us all and the important thing is to awaken it. We are here to better understand why we should accept Christ and revive His true teachings. Christ is within and if we delve deeply enough into the teachings of Christ we find that He indeed gave us the guidance to awaken and to enter the kingdom of heaven within.

Chapter 4 - Identifying with the Savior

If you would emulate the one who is known as the Son of God, be masterful as He; mastering the self, illusion, and the world you would not only be not a follower of Christ, you become Christ.

Like countless others, I spent most of my life trying to bridge the gap between religion and what I perceived as true spirituality. It was not until I made the shift in awareness and understanding to Christ though that I was able to cross that bridge. There is the church, there are multiple sects and denominations within the church, and there is Christ for whom the concept of church did not yet even exist. Christ *was* the church through the life He lived, the followers He encouraged, the teachings He shared and the acts He performed in the love of God.

Identifying with the Savior is really where Christ comes in. Becoming the type of consciousness that is not only willing to lead a life of devotion to God but to goodness and charity are the characteristics needed. Not only identifying with the teachings but with the consciousness that is capable of this so that we become the very essence of Christ within us all.

If everyone who professes to be a Christian actually emulated Christ and his teachings every day, we would live in a completely different world.

What would Jesus do? We have heard that question before but who really acts on it in day-to-day situations? Some do yes, but not enough. Poverty and hunger, sickness and despair, hopelessness, war and killing, child pornography and slave trade, so many senseless issues that stain humanity, deprive the soul and foul our well-being as well as that of the entire planet and all life upon it; all issues (and these being just a few) that Christ would completely eradicate. Issues that He would die for, as He did then and would still have to today because we sit idly by thinking one day He will return and fix it all. No. He lives in each of us and the only way He has to fix this messed up world is through our thoughts, actions, generosities, kindnesses and love. This is His hope for humanity, this is how He is the Savior, through our willingness to allow His work to be done through us as the instruments of love.

There is a couple my husband and I have seen a time or two recently. They walk by out on the street to and from the grocery store. They are very sad, lost and perhaps ill or on chemicals of some kind. They walk in a zombie-like state, their eyes are glassed over, they stare straight ahead, and they see or acknowledge nothing or no one. They are dressed shabbily, maybe an old Army jacket on one of them. They carry their grocery bags as they carry the burdens of a difficult life. They are middle aged, weary, tired and possibly close to destitute.

The first time I saw them, I whispered to my husband, "I hope we don't look that pitiful," only half joking, as we walked passed them.

They almost frightened me because we could have been only a step or two away from where they are (there but for the grace of God go I, right?). We had lost everything material due to foreclosure and bad economy and they are a reminder of where we could have, or still could, land. Yet even with as much as we lost materially, our souls soared higher than ever as we clung to our faith and to our beliefs and followed what we knew to be the chosen path.

It was not the state of their finances that worried me as much as the state of their souls. They seem deserted, devoid of Spirit, of life. I can handle being poor to a point but the loss of soul is frightening indeed. Who knows what sadness, difficulties or horrors have been allowed to rob them of their most precious treasure? Or perhaps they gave their souls over in ignorance to the evils of drugs or alcohol. Either way, they seemed devoid of any Spirit or natural being. They are shadow people;

those we avoid, those we also refuse to acknowledge or accept, for they are threats to our very way of life. They represent everything we wish to push away, to turn our eyes from and ignore. If we do not see them, they do not exist, or so we try to convince our ego. They are also the shadows of you and me. Shadows cast off from our own existence. They are our shadows living in the darkness of a world we dare not even imagine.

The second time I saw them though, I instinctively blessed them. My heart felt their pain even though their numbness may keep them from feeling it. I so want them to heal and find joy, love and beauty in their life. I sent them all the love and well-being that they as human beings so deserve. Though I may wind up even poorer than they, I no longer fear them for they showed me that Christ works through us all whether or not we are aware of it, if only we are willing and able to see. Because however we choose to respond to others is how we are responding to Christ, for He walks within us all. The gift they gave me was worth more than any blessing I could bestow as it was the gift of the appreciation of life and of cherishing the infinite soul with which we have been blessed. For as it says in Matthew 25:40 (KJV), "And the King shall answer and say unto them, Verily I say unto you, Inasmuch as ye have done it unto one of the least of these my brethren, ye have done it unto me."

ChristianBibleReference.org states regarding the teachings of Christ, "In His sermons and parables, Jesus seeks to shock us out of our selfishness and worldliness and create in us a true passion for the welfare of our fellow men, women and children around the world. Universal love is at the very heart of Jesus' teachings; it is God's earthly work for us. What matters to God is our love for Him and our love for each other. Wealth, power and status count for nothing in the kingdom of God. When we truly love our neighbors, we do our part to make the world a better place, and we find our own fulfillment in life."

Christ was the threshold for new beginnings to teach and to summon those with understanding along his way.

"Jesus, for example, can be regarded as a man who by dint of austerities and meditation attained wisdom; or on the other hand, one may believe that a god descended and took upon himself the enactment of a human career. The first view would lead one to imitate the master literally, in order to break through, in the same way as he, to the transcendent, redemptive experience. But the second states that the hero is rather a symbol to be contemplated rather than an example to be literally followed. The divine being is a revelation of the omnipotent Self, which dwells within us all. The contemplation of the life thus should be undertaken as a meditation on one's own immanent divinity, not as a prelude to precise imitation, the lesson being not 'Do thus and be good,' but 'Know this and be God.'" (Joseph Campbell, The Hero with a Thousand Faces. p. 275)

So it is not really to imitate Christ but to *be* Christ; through Christ we become God in the flesh and in our actions. As we are also told in Galatians 2:20 (KJV) "I am crucified with Christ: nevertheless I live; yet not I, but Christ liveth in me: and the life which I now live in the flesh I live by the faith of the Son of God, who loved me, and gave himself for me." (Paul is speaking)

What Christ was trying to teach is that Christian divinity lies within each of us. It is our job to open to it to receive and to allow the flow to come forth.

Not only do we need to do as Christ but we need to *be* as Christ. He has given us the love, caring and compassion in our hearts to do this but we must open to receive it and then we must do the work here on Earth. Christ spent time in solitude and Spirit but He also spent time out in the world; healing, helping and giving. Balance is a key. We are both spiritual and physical and we need to be both to fully experience the magic of life.

There is no balance left in Christianity. Many Christians focus more on the idea that Christ died for our sins than actually living the teachings. He said that His Father sent him to save the world. The world was to be saved through His *teachings*, through belief on Him.

It seems that so many have focused so much on the idea that He died for their sins that they have turned away from the teachings thinking all they merely have to do is accept Him as their savior and they are good to go. The heck with all that love and compassion and giving and sharing. How twisted it has all become. Christ was here to teach us love. If He was the embodiment of anything, it was love; love straight from God Himself, from the Creator, the Father, and *that* is the message we were supposed to receive. Love as Christ. Though it is important to honor His death, we must bring back the balance by honoring His life and following His teachings. We need to identify with the savior through His teachings and allow Him to resurrect within.

Chapter 5 - Experiencing the Change

Awakening is Three-Fold, a Triad.
Awakening to Self, Awakening to Christ,
Awakening to Life.

The meaning of the word awaken is obvious: to wake up, to stop sleeping. This then is applied as a metaphor in spiritual principles.

Taking a look at the root word from the Old English *awæcnan*, means "to spring into being. (Dictionary.com)

Awaken is generally applied to the awakening of the Spirit within us, to the spiritual realm, to our consciousness, but it is not limited to this. This is only one part of the full awakening. There is also an awakening to self, and there is an awakening to life. These three awakenings may occur in any order depending upon the individual's circumstances, psychological baggage and various triggers throughout a person's life. My own personal experience has been self – Spirit – life.

Awakening to Self

To awaken to self means that we become aware of our existence. We begin to wonder who we are, where we came from and why we are here. This can lead to thoughts of where we will go from here which with some people may translate to the bigger picture, the spiritual realm and thoughts of the afterlife. But in the self-awakening we begin to experience feelings, thoughts and notions of our own self-awareness. We begin to see our flaws and dig deeper to alleviate the negative, heal our wounds, and let go of our painful baggage. We become aware of our behavior as a person, realizing this affects our own self as well as others and through this we become aware of how we treat others. We begin to heal and change. We begin to treat our self and others with respect and are concerned for well-being.

Awakening to the Spirit

Awakening to the Spirit is an opening to receive Christ, a union within of the self and the Divine. Many things in life may trigger this type of awakening, it depends upon the individual because we are each evolving at our own spiritual growth rate. To some it comes easy, to some it comes harder, and to some perhaps it never comes at all, but this is our goal, this is our aim for growth and enlightenment as souls and as physical representations of God. Through this spiritual awakening we come to develop compassion, love, gratitude, an eye for beauty and a heart for all of life which leads to the awakening to life.

Awakening to Life

Awakening to life really does mean to spring to life; to come alive, suddenly seeing and taking in all that is around you, fully participating in all of the beauty, pain and glory that is life. Life in the physical. Savoring each moment and being in the present. Appreciating the gift that has been so graciously bestowed upon us to experience the physical as spiritual beings; allowing the Holy Spirit, the life force, to experience each tender moment on earth. Smelling the air, walking on the sand, holding a newborn, tasting the foods we eat.

The joys and experiences of waking to life are countless and when this occurs, we have a new zest, energy to share and interact with others, and to see and experience our world for what it is. We appreciate all life; we want to help and to give back because we are now aware of how blessed that we are in the physical world and appreciative of all that we have been given. God resides within everything that is in the physical world so it is understandable that once we have awoken spiritually that we come to the life-awakening and the balance of all that is between self, Spirit and life.

The combination of the self-awakening, the spiritual-awakening and life-awakening, make the complete process three-fold. This tri-nature could be applied to the Trinity or Triad of the Father, Son and Holy Ghost with awakening as self being the Son or the Spirit incarnate, the Father as the spiritual awakening when we open and connect to the Father of All, the Creator or Spirit within, and thirdly the awakening of life relating to the Holy Ghost as the Spirit is within all of life. When we have completed the three phases, we have then had a full awakening. Within this full awakening we will then continue to grow and evolve in Christ through the physical toward the life that has been willed for us.

Receiving Christ is what it means to be re-born or born again "Jesus answered and said unto him, Verily, verily, I say unto thee, Except a man be born again, he cannot see the kingdom of God." John 3:3 – (KJV)

Our consciousness must awaken, must be re-born into His spirit. Inside the center of the suffering lies a joy spot. When you find it, you are freed. This is pure bliss. The way to the spot is through mindful prayer, meditation, focus, breath, will and calm. This is the point at which you have reached your maximum for pain and are open enough to reach for the joy.

God cannot do it for you, you still have to make up your mind and do the work. But you will be given the strength and support that you need. With sincerity and determination, you will break through. Spending time each day in prayer, meditation and reflection will aid you tremendously in your growth and even more so if you are experiencing hardships.

What we have to understand is that God is not outside of us, God lives within each of us, and though God is also outside in every single thing, God is also within and it is this strength that is there and available to draw upon but we have to actually open the connection and do the drawing. We tend to say a prayer and then become frustrated when nothing occurs. This is because there is work to do on our end as well. Many times we may be receiving the answer but we are not open to seeing it. Other times it may require action on our part to complete the answer, the transaction. Other times our desires are not manifested or prayers seemingly unanswered because although we have free will, once we are on God's path for our life, He is in charge of the what, how and when.

If we have given our life to God, God gives us free will yes but within the realm of the choices laid out on His path for us. If He does not want us to do something and we are on a spiritual path, no matter how much visualization or mental power we put into it, it is not going to happen, and sometimes we have to accept that. God has reasons for the events in our lives; they are our lessons, tests and servitude. All these attitudes about creating our own destiny are not on the path of God because in doing this, when we try to force-create our own destiny, we are working against God's plan for us. Once again, this is IF you have given your life to God. Those who have not given their life to God may visualize and see their desires materialize with effort but these efforts are not focused on God's plan for them.

Christ tells us in the Sermon on the Mount, Matthew 6:7-8, "But when ye pray, use not vain repetitions, as the heathen do: for they think that they shall be heard for their much speaking. 8 Be not ye therefore like unto them: for your Father knoweth what things ye have need of, before ye ask him." (KJV)

Your path is now the path of Christ. This does not mean there will not still be trials or difficulties. There will always be difficulties but this time you will face them with a renewed faith, purpose and understanding. Most of us do not get through life unscathed. We experience pain, sorrow, loss, heartbreak, death, divorce, illness, bullying, alienation, lack, and so many other negative experiences. These experiences all contribute to the person we become and they can contribute in positive or negative ways depending on how we allow them to affect us. I know that from a place of darkness, it sounds impossible to find joy, light or beauty in some or any of these or other circumstances, but that is our challenge and it is possible. All things are possible with Christ. Trials and difficulties can also though cause blocks to Christ.

A big block in healing with Christ can be grief. If we are not dealing with it properly or at all, it will create a blockage between us and our connection to Him. We may even think that through prayer we are dealing with it but we are not. Grief brings pain and suffering, right? That is our theory. If we are in connection we truly can turn these over to God but it does not just magically happen, we have to do the letting go, we have to make the shift in perception. We have to make up our mind to come out of the darkness and to remain there, not turning back when the next crisis threatens to take us back there again. If you have remained in connection, when the next crisis occurs, you will be able to maintain or re-gain a positive and joyful position but you still have to do the work, you have to make it happen. We can grieve without suffering. We can extend love, understanding, and heartfelt feelings to the person or cause of the grief but we do not have to make our own selves suffer. We do not have to wallow in it, as much as we may want to.

Christ was compassionate to all who suffered. Imagine dealing with the multitudes and not letting all of that suffering get you down. Is it possible to find beauty in suffering, love in pain? It has to be there because everything exists in balance. We cannot have one without the other but finding one within the other can be difficult. It is a matter of perception and compassion.

This is where a shift in perception is necessary. If someone is in pain and suffering, if you are in a compassionate state, the beauty is that their suffering has caused you to feel and experience the beauty of love and compassion toward them. In their own state of suffering, or if you are suffering, the switch in perception is to see that your suffering was not in vain, that it was given to another for growth toward love and compassion. It is give and take on both parts and most of us will experience each scenario in a lifetime. It is up to us to find the beauty in the lesson and keep it in our heart.

Staying in the moment is not only one of the steps to staying with Christ but will also get you through any storm, even if you have to take it one minute, one moment, at a time. Stay focused on the moment, breathe in and exhale and give yourself the command to reach the place of Christ within. Call upon Him to calm the storm and He will.

God asks different things of each of us in regard to our faith, devotion, growth, and lessons to be learned. Sometimes these may seem extreme or unfair in comparison to others who seemingly have less struggles, obstacles or despair.

In my case, I was stripped of everything material in my life; left with only the basic necessities and my faith, receiving the day-to-day needs provided in order that I might further my growth and enlightenment. Would you release everything material for your spiritual devotion? I hope that you are never faced with that question, and had I been outright asked, it would have been difficult to near-impossible to answer with an absolute yes. Conditioning, creature-comforts, and just downright selfishness, are difficult to override when faced with that question. God knew this about me yet also knew my sincere desire for spiritual evolution and determined the outcome for me; an outcome which I could not have managed of my own conscious will.

I have spent much time in thought of the sisters and monks, yogis and masters, who live, or have lived, in isolation through spiritual devotion. I have researched monastic life and much that it entails. Previous research has led me to the gothic meandering halls of medieval abbeys while tracing the footsteps of the likes of Hildegard von Bingen or St. Francis of Assisi and this helped to give me a sense of spiritual discipline which I would soon need.

As fate would have it after losing everything financially, going on the road in an RV seemed the simplest solution; winding finally into a small park in an isolated mountain town. The park felt much like a cloister; the RV a cell (and I mean cell in the usage that in a monastery, the devotee's small and simple room is referred to as a cell). There is a monastery not too far away, up in the mountains, where the Benedictine monks live quietly and harmoniously, self-sufficiently and in continual devotion, to which I have visited. Many is the quiet morning back in my own cloister as I hear the birds singing and see the mist move over the mountains, that I imagine what it would feel like to waken high in the quiet cells of the monastery, in almost complete isolation from the physical world. They are so immersed in the natural world with nothing but the monk and God as one, and God and nature as one, monk and nature as one.

When the seeker is at this point, whether in the isolation of monastic life or in whatever circumstance fate has placed him, he (or she) has nothing left but the path itself, and all distractions are removed, then a miraculous metamorphosis occurs. When the day-to-day clutter is cleared, the outer noise silenced, one begins to look inside the self in the truest search for God and finds Christ thusly waiting there within. The whole is within, and the whole is without, yet we are within the whole and the whole is within us. It is a miraculous discovery.

Your path and lessons to this discovery will be different from mine, but if you are earnest in your search, the path will be there, sometimes whether you are consciously ready and fully willing or not. We can be brought to a personal brink of destruction in that our eyes may be opened, our sight restored.

Matthew 9:28 (KJV), "When He had gone indoors, the blind men came to Him, and He asked them, 'Do you believe that I am able to do this?' 'Yes, Lord,' they replied. 29 Then He touched their eyes and said, 'According to your faith will it be done to you.' 30 And their sight was restored." This teaching implies that our level of faith is a determining factor in the receipt of our spiritual sight. It is therefore the sometime warranted reason for extenuating or extreme circumstances that will strengthen our faith, thereby leading us to the fullest restoration possible.

Are we all born into the light and the darkness then ekes its way in, or are we born into the darkness and must struggle and learn our way to the light? This is a philosophical question and open for thought and debate. I think that we are born into the light and then must continually battle the ever-encroaching darkness that threatens to overtake us if we do not remain in awareness. Once we lose our awareness, it is then that the need to be re-born or to re-awaken arises. We are all children of God, the Spirit resides within each but if we allow the darkness to overtake our consciousness, if we shut out or turn away from our connection to the Spirit, then though we are children of God, that does not automatically ensure the deathly passage into the light of the Divine. Though we are all children of God, we must awaken to God within us, within our hearts and minds and live our lives thus. The murderer or rapist is a child of God but his God consciousness has been blocked off therefore simply being a child of God is not enough. It was Christ's sacrifice and true nature that brought to us the way to unlock this passage. John 14:6 (KJV), "Jesus saith unto him, I am the way, the truth, and the life: no man cometh unto the Father, but by me," which may be interpreted as without accepting Christ, no one will be in conscious union with God.

As written in 1 Corinthians 6:19, "What? know ye not that your body is the temple of the Holy Ghost [which is] in you, which ye have of God, and ye are not your own? 20 For ye are bought with a price: therefore glorify God in your body, and in your spirit, which are God's." (KJV) and, 2 Corinthians 5:17 – "Therefore if any man [be] in Christ, [he is] a new creature: old things are passed away; behold, all things are become new." This is living as Christ.

Whether or not you believe that Christ was the literal son of God or you believe Christianity to include metaphor, receiving the consciousness is the point because either way you look at it; it is one and the same principle. God (the Father, the Spirit) beget His Son, Christ, with a higher understanding to bring forth and share with the world. Christ was the first to understand and literate these concepts into understanding for the layman and Christ was born and died to initiate this change.

There are many translations for the Bible verse, 2 Corinthians 5:17. "Therefore if any man [be] in Christ, [he is] a new creature: old things are passed away; behold, all things are become new." (KJV). The Bible is, and always has been, open to interpretation as demonstrated in International Standard Version, of John 3:16, "For this is how

God loved the world: He gave his unique Son so that everyone who believes in him might not be lost but have eternal life," which places an entirely different context onto the verse with the use of the word "unique" verses the King James version which says, "For God so loved the world, that he gave his *only* begotten Son, that whosoever believeth in him should not perish, but have everlasting life." I think that we can all agree on *unique* regardless of our perception or level of understanding. Christ certainly was unique; unique in the way that He incarnated as a person with a gift with which He was born to share with the world, our salvation.

Let us keep in mind that Christianity did not yet exist with all its dogma, arguments, perceptions and misconceptions, nor was it Christ's aim. The goal was simple: share the truth so that others too would be able to come into the God's kingdom.

Our mistake is in perceiving God as an external source and divinity when truly He already resides within us; it is simply up to us to open to receive Him. There is no need to reinvent the wheel but there is a need to reinvent our perception of that wheel. In truth, there are as many perceptions of Christ as there are people to perceive but most perceptions are based on what, to many, are the surface beliefs and interpretations without any individual thought or search into the deeper meanings.

Another change we will experience in accepting Christ is removing judgment. There is an innate ability within us to judge. We have to be able to assess any situation, moment, or person in life in order to make the best and safest decision. However, it is very easy for ego and piety to run rough-shod over this mechanism and it is something that we must continually monitor so that we do not become overly judgmental and in this process become discriminating based on the wrong or self-righteous judgments. The innate ability to judge is there for our well-being, perseverance and survival. Like eating to stay alive, it is a primitive instinct. It is to be used as a positive tool from which to learn and should produce the best ideal outcome. It is not meant to be used to judge others or to discriminate against others based on biased or false judgments.

An easy way to repair an overly judgmental attitude once identified is to remember that we are Christ living and experiencing life in physical form and that when we judge anyone or anything, we can choose to act as Christ would. We would do well to remember, Matthew 7:1-3, "Judge not, that ye be not judged. 2 For with what judgment ye judge, ye shall be judged: and with what measure ye mete, it shall be measured to you again. 3 And why beholdest thou the mote that is in thy brother's eye, but considerest not the beam that is in thine own eye?" (KJV)

Being overly judgmental can also cause a block in our own expression and development if we are making judgments inaccurately about ourselves due to wrongly perceived or negative aspects of our nurturing environment. We can be overly judgmental of our selves, trying to keep our self in a mold and therefore hindering our true self's expression and that is after all, why we are here, to allow God to express and experience through us. When we are awakened to Christ, He is acting within us and this then brings us to the desire to act for the love of God.

How much in our day is done for the love of God? With the exception of those in the clergy or monastic life or some in communal situations, for the most part it is very little, if any. Most people do their one hour of attending service a week then go back to day-to-day life. What we have to look at here is how we can turn the day-to-day into acts that reflect our spiritual being, how we can be more Christ-like in our daily living and this is two-fold: attitude and action.

What are your attitudes and actions today, every day, toward others? Do they reflect Christ? Our attitudes and actions should be for the love of God and through this touching and helping everyone we meet and everything we do in the day-to-day. It really is all about attitude.

Obviously we cannot all go live in a monastery or commune, we have to have jobs and livelihood, but what we must do is have the right attitude. Ask for the right life and the right attitude and you will know the grace of God. The right life does not though in any way denote the easy path. That is a mistake that many spiritual seekers make in the beginning, including myself. Sometimes, many times, the trials and difficulties can be even greater, all the while we are thinking, why me, I chose the path of righteousness, I am on the path for God, while others are having a seemingly easy time of it all. That is the point though isn't it, for the love of God? We must be open to seeking the lessons God would have us learn and through this developing the right attitude and keeping to our commitment to give, share and care. God will help you reach the point wherein when you do something, it is for the love of God, pure and simple.

Consider Christ's attitude amidst those who scoffed. We are conditioned to succumb to peer-pressure. We tend to think of peer pressure in terms of adolescence or teens but in truth as adults we do not pass from it. We are pressured at every turn we make, in every thought we think, to conform, to be successful in society's eyes, in so many ways that it would constitute a book in itself. Suffice it to say for now that this unbending need to follow the pack is in its greatest folly, attitude.

Christ said: 9 "After this manner therefore pray ye: Our Father which art in heaven, Hallowed be thy name.
10 Thy kingdom come, Thy will be done in earth, as it is in heaven.
11 Give us this day our daily bread.
12 And forgive us our debts, as we forgive our debtors.
13 And lead us not into temptation, but deliver us from evil: For thine is the kingdom, and the power, and the glory, for ever. Amen." Matthew 6:9-13 (KJV)

In recent prayer, after coming out of years of trying times, confusion, uncertainty and fear, when I finally was so stripped down that there was nothing left but to seek peace, to seek love, to seek God's union, God said to me, *"I have held everything for you until you are clear."*

At this point I really understood that one must seek God for God's sake, for the pure love and essence of God; not because of fear or pear pressure or wanting something, but only for the sake of God, then and only then will all be revealed. It took a long time but I finally wanted that connection, in all sincerity, just for the sake of it, without anything else; minus fear, destitution or desire, and that is why I heard that voice and when I did, I went from hoping to knowing with a full understanding of the God-connection. The bottom line is that you have to want to know God. George Harrison's, *My Sweet Lord,* comes to mind, "I really want to know you, I really want to be with you . . . "

Receive the Spirit in gladness and let it come through in all you do.

Our intuitive power, the knowing within us *is* God. Many people spend their lives closed off from this communication though it may still seep through into their consciousness with inklings here or there such as getting a feeling not to do a specific thing or that the phone is going to ring. But it takes continued effort to open and fully clear the channels so that He may flow freely through us in all of our daily activity and thought. Three sure ways to open these channels are with prayer, meditation and being in nature. The more effort we put into connecting with and allowing the flow God, the stronger we will become spiritually and the closer we come to our true purpose and goal: allowing Him to experience the physical through us and being of the spiritual consciousness when at last we cross over, for it is the love we will take with us in an open heart into His eternity.

Open your heart to love. It always sounded good but in a way seemed cliché to me and to be honest, I just did not get it. What was I to do? How was I to open up? I thought I was (don't we always?). What was I doing wrong?

Then one day I felt a flood of strong spiritual love, for the Spirit, for God. I realized how much I love the Spirit and that's why I try my best every day to put that out into words and visuals to share with others. And in feeling my own love of God, I felt His love for me. Though I focused on it, prayed for it, I could never feel it because I never felt it. I had to open to the love first. I had never allowed myself to open to it. I guess I thought it would just come to me and maybe in a way it did but still I had to open to letting myself feel love before I could receive it.

This is a big step in our ability to heal; when we can love again, when we can open our hearts to love again. And there are many traumatic or hurtful things that can block us from loving; it does not just have to be a failed or broken love relationship. It can be grief and loss, pride or poverty, illness or family issues, physical abuse or drug addiction or any one of a number of things that cause us to wall our self off, not only from loving others but from loving God.

After this experience of receiving God's love, I saw this quote which aptly summed it up:

"True love is a state of consciousness, the highest that a human being can attain, it is Divine consciousness in all its fullness. Those who are touched by this love even for an instant, feel as if they have been struck by lightening. Suddenly they receive something so sublime, that they almost cannot bear it, but it is this love which enlightens them, which vivifies and re-awakens them." (Omraam)

God cannot get through until we allow Him to, in whatever form you believe. This is what it really means to open your heart to love. Allow yourself to love and you will be moved and loved by Him. God's love is always there for us, but we cannot feel or receive it until we open within, until we open our hearts to love and when we do, we will experience the change.

There are many changes to be experienced once Christ has been accepted. Stay centered, keep the path open and be for the new and loving changes ahead.

Chapter 6 - Turning Things Around

One question we hear frequently is why does God allow this or why does God allow that? God does not allow, we do. We have a choice to become better people. We have a choice to help our neighbor or the hungry; we have a choice to be kind and accepting, Why does God allow these wars, starvation, crimes, illnesses? God does not allow them, we do.

God does not do right or wrong, that is up to us as humans to choose. It is up to each of us to do the right thing; that is what God wants, to see us become loving beings who make the right choices and when we do, thereby raising the collective conscious to the God-level which is the second coming of Christ. This is the reason why prayer works and the more praying, the better. Prayer is our consensus to allow the Him to work through us and in doing this we bring forth a channel for the power of manifestation into each others' lives. This must be done freely, from the individual at a conscious level, to have an effect at the collective level. It is at the collective level that through prayer, we can move mountains.

Religious extremism and world religious events, both in the present and in the past two-thousand years, should be enough to awaken our sensitivities and intellect to the truth of the teachings of Christ and the need for a collective understanding of what these really mean. Regardless of which religious text or segment through which these timeless teachings are perceived, if the truth is not followed, it becomes twisted and thusly removed from its point of origin: which is to evolve spiritually, to live our lives as decent, loving, compassionate and giving human beings.

"But seek first the kingdom of God and his righteousness, and all these things will be added to you." Matthew 6:33 (KJV)

We cannot move toward a collective awakening until we move individually. We cannot move forward individually until we are living right and have received the truth of Christ within. When we are worthy of the truth, we receive the truth. So much is not as it is perceived. I can share only so much for it must be found within. We must be working toward our awakening and living the life that God offers us through Christ as we move toward the light. Shift from the ego and material obsession must occur. Mindfulness and learning to live in the moment are two of the most important factors in initiating the shift, as is the true desire to seek God and live the life that we are destined to live. *We* must make this choice. "For the gate is narrow and the way is hard that leads to life, and those who find it are few." Matthew 7:14 (ESV)

Many people do live Godly lives within the frame of their religion but they are not the majority. The majority believe that attending services or repeating the platitudes are all they need do. Man cannot know God until he has spent time with Him within through contemplation, reflection, meditation and prayer. It is a continuing ongoing commitment that must always be nurtured to keep the mind clear, pure and focused. "Blessed are those who do His commandments that they may have the right to the tree of life, and may enter through the gates into the city." Revelations 22:14 (KJV)

We must learn to care for others as Christ did. He cannot return until we do, until we become a caring, loving human race as a whole, at least as a majority so that in effect, the shift will begin to occur. Though He may well return physically as scripture tells us, for now, the return is within each of us, within our hearts and minds. When all prejudice is gone, when we have fed and cared for the hungry and the sick, the poor, when crime and greed no longer control the hearts of men, then in

His most infinite Spirit, He will return in the name and light of love, within us.

Let us bring our hearts, minds and spirits together and lift our consciousness to Christ that we may heal and enlighten humanity.

In our daily lives, as we reach a new consciousness and awakening, there are many things that we can do to contribute to the growth, experience and expansion of our consciousness. In turn, as our consciousness expands, we will naturally begin to do these things.

Do things slowly and with awareness, doing so totally changes everything and brings Christ into each movement.

Make the time for a daily prayer practice, even if only five minutes a day. This will clear the mind, open the channels and soon you will find yourself connecting and staying longer as you experience Christ and the oneness of God.

In turning things around, changing our attitude to one of caring and giving while releasing the me-mentality that is so prevalent in our societies today, is the biggest step we can make in our individual and worldly transformation. Little changes make a big difference. Today most people get their attitude from the media and not from God. If everyone had a God-attitude, there really wouldn't be any world hunger, wars, or any other of the problems we face.

Following are some suggestions to help you begin to shift toward a quietened mind and life in Christ:

Contemplation and prayer. This is a most important time for your spiritual growth. Quiet, reflective time with God is crucial to your development.

Turn off the media and news. It is more necessary than ever to turn off the media, filter all that is going into your head. Just because it is in the media does not mean it is a truth for you to accept. Give yourself a break each day and leave the chaos behind. This includes social media.

Spend time in nature. We are natural beings and we need time in the sun, fresh air, near water if possible. Find some beauty in which to sit or walk. At least go outside. Being in nature is being with God. Nature stimulates our inner spirit, refreshes our tired minds and activates the muses for creativity.

Help those less fortunate. Find a way to help someone each day. Don't just hurry by thinking someone else will do the helping, be the one who does.

Silence. Stop talking. Any time spent in silence will aid your growth. No influences, no distractions, just you and your thoughts or no thoughts.

Listen, to others, to self, to God. We are always in too big of a hurry to listen to others, to God. Slow down and listen to what is being said. Hear the other person; hear the God-voice within.

Ask Christ for guidance in your life, on your path and with the day-to-day. You will always be guided positively in the best direction for your growth, well-being and divine purpose.

Keep an open mind. A closed mind dismisses the full human experience. Like the blossoming of a flower, an open mind engages fully in the experience of life. Allow your mind to open to new ways and understandings that will improve your spiritual growth.

Think for yourself. Stop listening to others, to the media, to false prophets, to propaganda and the likes. Listen to God.

Do as much as possible to keep yourself in a spiritual state of mind. We are not all born to be monks, we have to live and function in a fast-paced world but we do not have to fall for the marketing, succumb to the temptations, or insert ourselves into the negativity that flows unchecked.

It is time to reconnect to Christ, and in this light to the mind of Christ. He is risen within us and the path to follow is of His light. Living in this light is to allow the Spirit to work through us, through the physical, that we may help others and live to our fullest capacity.

Chapter 7 - Rationing the Word

Christ as the word is *Logos, b*reath as the word.

Ration – use sparingly, control, giving out, sharing, distributing' Latin from *ratio*, for reason. (Wikipedia.org)

The more widespread a teaching or philosophy becomes, the more deluded it becomes and this is especially the case with Christianity as multitudes of varies segments have broken away from the initial body. No longer pure, with this thinning of the teachings comes muddied water.

The Greek for *word* is "discourse" or "reason, the Logos conception derives from the opening of the Gospel of John and is often simply translated into English as: "In the beginning was the Word, and the Word was with God, and the Word was God."

Christ as the Logos

"As the Logos, Jesus Christ is God in self-revelation (Light) and redemption (Life). He is God to the extent that he can be present to man and knowable to man.

The paradox that the Logos is God and yet it is in some sense distinguishable from God is maintained in the body of the Gospel. That God as He acts and as He is revealed does not "exhaust" God as he is, is reflected in sayings attributed to Jesus: I and the Father are one and also, "the Father is greater than I." The Logos is God active in creation, revelation, and redemption. Jesus Christ not only gives God's Word to us humans; he is the Word." (Wikipedia.org)

Speaking of the word, or words, this may seem trivial but our use of words, especially the negative, must change. The more we awaken, the more we will understand this and begin to govern our thoughts and verbiage.

Sh@#, dang, darn, damn, f&@$, SOB, MF, GD, and so on. What do you think when you hear these words? How do they make you feel? Do you use them? Are you even aware when you use them? They are all negative but our language(s) have become so slack and filled with them that we may not even realize the negativity we are allowing.

Every time we cuss, we are putting out negative energy and we are doing it deliberately so that anyone around will know that we are in a negative mood. By allowing ourselves to be in a mood that has to verbally express itself through cussing is not acting in Christ. Many of us cuss for different reasons. We curse to be cool, to get attention, out of anger, out of pain (who is not tempted when smashing a finger with a hammer or stumping an unsuspecting toe?) out of habit, out of ignorance, out of cultural environment. We may also try to put an explanation point on a statement or thought in a language wherein we have lost the ability to make our point intelligently or others have lost the ability to listen intelligently. Frustration, or impatience may also be a factor, or to actually damn the person or thing to which we refer. Whatever our reasons, it is better for our soul and the energy we are projecting toward others to refrain and instead think, verbalize and project light, love and heartwarming feelings through our choice of words, because when we are in Christ, we are speaking for Christ, for God within.

Every word that we speak is on the breath of God, therefore every word we speak is sacred, or should be, as is every breath we take.

In Hinduism, Om is the breath of God, the vibration and sound of God. In the Bible, 1 John, 1:1, "In the beginning was the Word, and the Word was with God, and the Word was God." (KJV). Some of the most ancient teachings tell us that indeed God is the breath and the word. "By the word (logos) of the Lord the heavens were made, and by the breath of his mouth all their host." Psalm 33:6 (ESV)

There is an entire school of thought around the concept of Christ as Logos (Greek: Λόγος, lit. "Word". – Wiki), yet language and speech are probably two of the things most taken for granted by the human race. Language is possibly one of the things most abused by humans. Most give little thought to the sacredness of this concept or understand that as we breathe and speak, we do so through the very grace of God, from the very life-spark of God.

This is a huge realization when you finally get it. It is almost overwhelming when once you realize that it is through God that we breathe and speak. We then see and understand the abuse and obstruction we have caused because we have not been aware of, or have been ignorant to, our own power through the God-source within us. In understanding this concept, we should then ration our use of words to those that are Christ-like, that are of God.

Many wise teachings also speak about the words of fools, and when we are unaware of our speech, we too are the fool. Understanding this and practicing this is a vital part of attaining a Christ-like mind and remaining there. It is imperative that we grasp the damage that words can do (as well as the blessing that words can be) to ourselves, to others, to our collective evolution at large and to God, for when we use damaging words, we are inhibiting God's ability to act within us. Thus, we are denying God! We are imposing ugliness onto something that is pure light and love. We are refusing the source its benign nature as our human ego controls our speech. We are then not allowing our self to act in Christ or Christ to act through us.

Rhetoric, manipulation, verbal abuse, and so many other ways of using speech negatively have disavowed God, Christ-inherent. We have defiled not only the beauty of our own speech and languages simply as cultural and human factors but as the transmitters for the good of ourselves, our loved ones and all others in the world, and the good of God. How much have we self-damaged ourselves, others and society simply through being unaware that every word is sacred? Becoming aware right now can end this misuse and put us on the track to the holy, compassionate and right use of the breath and speech as it is intended, as the breath and word of God.

You may have your Bible with you or near you today. I don't want you to open it, I want you to just hold it because I know that it may give you comfort. You too know that it gives you comfort but may not fully be aware of the why of this. You may consider the Bible to be *the word of God*. The word of God is the very breath and essence of God and this is why you may find comfort in that concept. If you meditate on these things, you will find them to be true as you feel the presence of God surrounding you and welling up inside of you. As you focus on the breath, on God, remember as John said, the *word* was God. The words contained in the Bible are yes, wise words from the pen of men, but men who allowed themselves to receive and speak the word of God. They were men who gave the Spirit free reign and were able to put forth the wisest teachings that have since provided comfort and direction for thousands of years.

What we are to focus upon here is the word as the breath itself of God, as it forms within you from the Holy Spirit and releases from you to travel and put forth its effects externally, just as did those who spoke for God and wrote for the Bible. For if God is the word and the word is the breath, then when you speak, you speak the word of God through the breath of God. This is where you need to reflect. This is from where you can truly derive comfort because you are the expression of God through the breath and the word and you can therefore create and extend comfort through these for yourself and others. Every breath and every word spoken by you are the breath and the word of God. This is an astounding revelation once understood.

Meditate on the word of God as you speak it, as He speaks through you and what you are allowing or disallowing Him to say. Understand that though this wisdom and comfort has been given you in a book through the words of others, so too is it given to *you* as you read those words. You only need be aware of this and get out of the way of the Holy Spirit when reading God's word.

Let it breathe, let it speak through you in every breath in every moment in every word that is spoken each day.

". . . out of the abundance of the heart the mouth speaketh." Matthew 12:34 (KJV)

Chapter 8 - Our Awakening World

As I mentioned in chapter two, all of our great world religions originated in the East. What was the rest of the world doing at that time? It is true, we *were* swinging from the trees as they say. We had not yet had any revelations or great teachings or teachers reveal themselves. Many cultures were still operating in earth-related understandings based on the cycles and seasons, agriculture and superstition (not necessarily always soul-based truths). There were sound teachings in these cultural beliefs yet as in the case of rural or indigenous peoples, were transmitted orally but in most cases, little was recorded

All-in-all, by the time the majority of the Western world did begin to open its eyes, these major religions had already begun to spread so that those residing in the western world began to absorb the dogma that had resulted from the original teachings. Indeed we did eventually begin to experience our own stage of enlightenment in the west, millennia later, such as the Renaissance, the origination of free-masonry and similar free-thinking groups, through the insightful writings of the Romantics, and eventually to the explosion of the free-thinking of the 1960s which turned into a worldwide revolution. But even with all of our western advancements, we are still babies, toddlers, in comparison to the great teachers and philosophies of the East and certainly, those of Christ. It would behoove us to redirect our attention to these teachings in their original form just as these teachers meant for them to be practiced. This includes the teachings of Christ for we, as westerners with all of our Christianity, have still yet to come anywhere near catching up to the correct practice and understanding of these great teachings. Now that we have internet, technology, and world-wide access, we can see, learn and understand more than ever and we can now catch up to timeless teachings.

As we catch up and reach new awareness, the mass consciousness begins to rise. Mass ascension is our rising (collective) consciousness in its truest form. The Christian apocalypse is in truth the dawn of Christ's reign, it is the coming time of enlightenment, of a mass awakening to Christ within.

As for the end of the world and Revelations, Christ said, in Mark 13:32, "But of that day and that hour knoweth no man, no, not the angels which are in heaven, neither the Son, but the Father."

The reign of darkness showered upon us by naysayers is going to end. We will shift to the positive, to love. When finally we achieve one love in the world, *then* Christ will have returned. The second coming is through love which perhaps then He will actually appear, if not, He will live within us. "Thou shalt love thy neighbor as thyself." Mark 12:31, is the second most important commandment according to Christ, second only to loving God, ans as He lives within us we will begin to love more and more, our brothers, sisters, and neighbors far and wide.

Those with condemnation in their hearts will not see the coming glory and light. Believing in the end times is sending condemnation to the world rather than seeking to fill the world and those in it with love, light, hope, and faith. It is to be a new time.

Coming into the light of Christ means awakening to the needs of others, the planet and all living beings. As we awaken into this consciousness, we begin to feel and experience the connectedness of all that is. It is impossible to awaken and not begin to feel and experience this. We realize and understand that what we do for others, we do through Christ for God. The more we do in this life, the further along our spiritual growth we are propelled for the time of the crossing over after this life into eternity. It is our duty to reach out to others in whatever way we are guided.

The underlying currents of the world are circling beneath us. Though prayer and unity in will help to control these currents and bring us toward a new universal and individual consciousness clearing the right-of-way to mankind's evolution, we must first fix ourselves. The world is filled with so many problems, so many wrongs. People think that they are helping by staying in a constant upset over the state of the world, always ranting and sharing bad news of all the problems. But this type of behavior does no good because it is not the multitude of problems that we must change, but rather the hearts and minds of people. When people change, the bad things will drop away, solutions will be found. When the hearts and minds of the populace are filled with love, then the changes will come. This type of behavior also breeds anger and anger does not accomplish tasks. Some share the problems they think need to be solved but many are doing so in anger. We must operate from the center; we must speak love. So unless we are sending out love, it does no good to complain of the atrocities. They may only be healed with love, and love requires awakening; awakening to Christ within, accepting Him and following His teachings. We must join together.

The otherworld is not broken down into segments per our cultural belief systems. It is not compartmentalized. Our eternity there may depend heavily on our humanly growth while here. Christ came with His teachings to assure our growth and to offer us the path.

The two most important lessons we can all learn are that it is really just about being happy each day and understanding that we are a part of it all, it is all connected. One of Christ's commandments was that we love one another as He loved us. We are all connected.

It is all connected, we are all connected, life is all connected. Spirituality and life are not two separate things; spirituality and the planet are not two separate things. All is one and one affects the other. What we do in this world allows God the opportunity to act through each and every one of us for the better for all and for His divine plan. Our hope should be that we will raise our collective consciousness to a state of enlightenment in caring for ourselves, each other, all life and the planet on which we live through Christ.

There is a shift in consciousness coming and those who do not make the shift are those who will be "left behind."

Conclusion

Obviously we cannot all drop what we are doing and go and live in communes or revert to living like the Amish though peaceful it may be. We have created a growing, evolving, thriving society of life that should, and will, continue to evolve *if* we take these teachings and apply them as they were meant to be applied, to create the world God so desired that Christ was sent and given these teachings to impart. Teachings which would (and still can) create a world full of peace and love and help for one another.

We are all just humans trying to make sense of what sometimes seems a messed-up place. We all have our talents and gifts and if we are following the Holy Spirit's path for us, we are using those gifts and talents to help others and to help make the world a better place to live while we achieve God's will for our lives.

In the divine process of illumination, a gathering of light will sound and the once dark protégé will suddenly find himself together with God, through Christ.

Whatever our hopes for the future, may they include the likeliness and mind of Christ, for it is through these that we will flourish as individuals and as a whole. There is love coming to the world, great love. Believe this. We are here to make it happen.

***

When this book was impressed upon me, I did not understand that I was first meant to live it, experience it, but now I have. If you can give Christ a fresh look with an open mind, I can attest from personal experience that it is not what you think it is nor will it be what you expected. It will be nothing short of a miracle as He leads you on, unfolding His mystery within your own life. He is patient, He is kind, He is loving and most of all, He is forgiving (for we know not what we do). Take yourself wholly and freely to His teachings with a fresh perspective, willing to learn and to receive. View Him not as the world views Him but as *He* reveals Himself to *you* through scripture, heart and prayer. I needed Him and I did not even know it. We all need Him. He is indeed the savior, and who among us does not need a savior? Every day that you are here, you are given another chance. Take it. Don't wait. Don't look back. Walk on into the light of Christ. Christ is cool. So much cooler than we ever thought. Toss out the old, in with the new, it is time for a new age of Christ within our hearts and within the world.

Made in the USA
Columbia, SC
11 September 2020